Seasons

Fall

Siân Smith

Heinemann Library
Chicago, Illinois

Editorial: Rebecca Rissman, Charlotte Guillain, and Siân Smith
Picture research: Elizabeth Alexander and Sally Claxton
Designed by Joanna Hinton-Malivoire
Printed and bound by South China Printing Company Limited

13 12 11 10 09
10 9 8 7 6 5 4 3 2 1

ISBN-13: 978-1-4329-2727-1 (hc)
ISBN-13: 978-1-4329-2732-5 (pb)

Library of Congress Cataloging-in-Publication Data
Smith, Siân.
  Fall / Siân Smith.
    p. cm. -- (Seasons)
  Includes bibliographical references and index.
  QB637.7.S65 2008
  508.2--dc22
                              2008049155

Acknowledgments
The author and publisher are grateful to the following for permission to reproduce copyright material: ©Alamy pp.**10**, **11** (Blend Images), **20** (David Norton), **9** (Judy Freilicher), **14**, **23 bottom** (Neil Dangerfield), **8** (Phill Lister), **16** (Renee Morris), **21** (Silksatsunrise Photography); ©Corbis pp.**22** (Craig Tuttle), **04 br** (Image100), **17** (Tetra Images), **04 tl** (Zefa/Roman Flury); ©GAP Photos pp.**18**, **23 top** (Fiona Lea); ©Getty Images pp.**04 tr** (Floria Werner), **5** (Philippe Renault); ©iStockphoto.com pp.**6**, **23 middle** (Bojan Tezak), **04 bl** (Inga Ivanova); ©Photodisc p.**12** (Photolink); ©Photolibrary pp.**13** (Chad Ehlers), **15** (J-Charles Gerard/Photononstop); ©Punchstock p.**7** (Brand X Pictures/Morey Milbradt); ©Shutterstock p.**19** (Vakhrushev Pavel).

Cover photograph of maple tree reproduced with permission of ©Shutterstock (Tatiana Grozetskaya). Back cover photograph reproduced with permission of ©Photodisc (Photolink).

Every effort has been made to contact copyright holders of any material reproduced in this book. Any omissions will be rectified in subsequent printings if notice is given to the publisher.

Contents

What Is Fall?

spring

summer

fall

winter

There are four seasons every year.

Fall is one of the four seasons.

When Is Fall?

spring

summer

winter

fall

The four seasons follow a pattern.

Fall comes after summer.

The Weather in Fall

It can be cooler in fall.

It can be foggy in fall.

9

What Can We See in Fall?

In fall we can see people in sweaters.

In fall we can see people in coats.

In fall we can see colored leaves
on trees.

12

In fall we can see colored leaves on the ground.

In fall we can see seeds.

In fall we can see fruits
and vegetables.

In fall we can see berries.

In fall we can see pumpkins.

In fall we can see bonfires.

In fall we can see fireworks.

In fall we can see animals carrying food.

In fall we can see birds flying away.

Which Season Comes Next?

Which season comes after fall?

Picture Glossary

bonfire outdoor fire

pattern happening in the same order

seed plants make seeds. Seeds grow into new plants.

Index

Note to Parents and Teachers
Before reading
Explain to children that there are four seasons every year: winter, spring, summer and fall.
Tell children that the seasons follow a pattern, or sequence. Write the four seasons on the
board and draw arrows showing their order. Show children that fall comes after summer.
Ask them what their favorite fall activities are.

After reading
Make a garland of leaves. You will need enough leaves from different trees for each child
to have one leaf; paper, pencils, crayons, scissors, and a long piece of string. Tell children to
select a leaf from your collection and to draw it on a piece of paper with a thick stem. They
should then mark the veins and cut out their leaf.
Fold the stem in half and attach it to the string. Suspend the string of leaves across
the classroom.

THE LIBRARY OF WHY?

Why Do Leaves Change Color?

Marian B. Jacobs, Ph.D

The Rosen Publishing Group's

PowerKids Press™

New York

For my grandsons, Carlos and Gianni.

Published in 1999 by The Rosen Publishing Group, Inc.
29 East 21st Street, New York, NY 10010

First Edition

Book Design: Danielle Primiceri

Photo Credits: Cover © 1996 PhotoDisc, Inc.; pp. 4, 11 © Richard H. Smith/FPG International; p. 7 © Telegraph Colour Library 1997/FPG International; p. 8 © Color Box 1992/FPG International; pp. 12, 15, 16, 20, 22 © 1996 PhotoDisc, Inc.; p. 19 © West, Larry/FPG International

Jacobs, Marian B.
    Why do leaves change color? / by Marian B. Jacobs.
        p. cm. — (The library of why?)
    Includes index.
    Summary: Provides answers to such questions about trees as "How do trees grow?", "How do trees change with the season?", and "How do leaves make food for the tree?"
    ISBN 0-8239-5275-4
    1. Trees—Miscellanea—Juvenile literature. 2. Leaves—Color—Miscellanea—Juvenile literature.
    [1. Trees—Miscellanea. 2. Leaves—Miscellanea. 3. Questions and answers.] I. Title. II. Series.
  QK475.8.J33 1998
  582.16—dc21   97–43893
                                                   CIP

Manufactured in the United States of America   AC

Contents

Why Are Leaves and Trees Important?

Trees are very important to life on Earth. They give us nuts, fruit, and maple syrup to eat. Trees are homes for animals such as birds and squirrels. Their **roots** (ROOTS) help keep soil from washing away. Trees give us **lumber** (LUM-ber) to build our houses and furniture.

Tree branches have leaves. Some trees have wide, flat leaves. Others have leaves that look like little needles. Leaves are very important because they make food for the tree and give off **oxygen** (AHK-sih-jen) that we breathe.

◀ Did you know that we make paper and pencils from trees?

What Are the Parts of a Tree?

A tree has three main parts: roots, a trunk, and leaves. The roots grow into the ground to hold the tree in place. The trunk supports the tree. Inside the trunk, there are two kinds of wood. The **sapwood** (SAP-wood) carries water from the roots to the leaves. Sapwood also carries food made in the leaves to all parts of the tree. Older sapwood hardens and becomes **heartwood** (HART-wood) which is what supports the tree. Outside the trunk are layers of bark. The outer bark protects the tree from insects and illness. Leaves hang on the branches. They make food for the tree.

6

Even though some trees may look different from others, they all have the same parts. ▶

LEAVES

SAPWOOD

OUTER BARK

INNER BARK

HEARTWOOD

CAMBIUM

ROOTS

How Do Trees Grow?

A tree grows higher by lengthening its twigs at the tips of its branches. At the ends of the twigs, buds add new growth.

The trunk and branches have a layer of **cells** (SELZ) called the **cambium** (KAM-bee-um). The cambium is between the inner bark and the sapwood. Every year the cambium adds a layer of new cells to the older wood. This makes the trunk and branches grow thicker. Each layer that grows forms a ring. You can tell how old a tree is by counting the rings inside its trunk.

◀ As a tree grows, it gets taller and wider.

How Do Trees Get Their Food?

Trees make their own food. They get some of the **ingredients** (in-GREE-dee-ints) they need from the soil. Tiny root hairs that grow out from the roots reach into the soil and take up water and **minerals** (MIH-ner-ulz). The water and minerals are carried up to the leaves by the sapwood. Trees get other ingredients, such as **carbon dioxide** (KAR-bin dy-OK-syd) gas from air, through their leaves. Leaves have special cells that use the ingredients and energy from the sun to make food. This is called **photosynthesis** (foh-toh-SIN-thuh-sis).

This oak tree has wide leaves to collect lots of sunlight. ▶

How Does Photosynthesis Work?

Leaves are sunlight collectors. They have cells that make a green coloring called **chlorophyll** (KLOR-uh-fil). Chlorophyll helps leaves absorb energy from sunlight. The leaves use this energy to mix carbon dioxide gas from the air with water from the soil. This mixture creates the food the tree needs to live. As the leaves go through the steps of photosynthesis, they give off oxygen into the air. Oxygen is very important to people. In fact, without oxygen in the air we would not be able to breathe.

◀ Photosynthesis can only work in green leaves.

How Do Trees Change with the Seasons?

Seasons change as Earth moves closer or farther from the sun. During fall, days get shorter and there is less sunlight. The ground gets colder and frost makes it harder for roots to take up water. Photosynthesis slows down and then stops. This causes leaves on **deciduous** (deh-SIH-joo-us) trees to change color and then fall to the ground. Spring comes when where you live gets closer to the sun. The ground warms up and spring rain makes water more available. Buds open into new leaves, and photosynthesis begins again.

Trees don't die in winter. They just rest until spring. ▶

Why Do Leaves Change Color In the Fall?

In the spring and summer, leaves look green because they contain chlorophyll. But leaves actually have other colors too, such as red, orange, and yellow.

The cells in leaves need sunlight for photosynthesis. When there is less sunlight, photosynthesis slows down. The chlorophyll slowly disappears. When chlorophyll is gone, the red, orange, and yellow colors can be seen. Maple trees turn red and orange, white birch trees glow yellow, and oak trees become reddish-brown.

◀ The trees in the northeastern United States are known for their bright and beautiful colors in fall.

How Do New Trees Grow?

In spring, trees blossom and in summer, they grow seeds. Seeds are the pits in fruits, such as apples and peaches. Nuts, such as acorns and walnuts, are also seeds. The seeds of evergreen trees are inside their cones. The cones open and drop their seeds to the ground where they may grow into new trees.

    Fruit and nuts fall to the ground when they are **ripe** (RYP). Some animals eat them as soon as they fall. Other animals bury nuts to eat later. These animals move the seeds around. Some seeds sprout and grow into new trees.

This seed may one day grow into a beautiful red oak tree. ▶

Why Are Evergreen Trees Green All Year?

Evergreen is a name given to trees that do not lose their leaves in fall. Most evergreens have leaves that look like needles. These needles have less water in them than the large, flat leaves on deciduous trees. This keeps them from freezing in cold weather.

Evergreen trees do not lose all of their needles at once, the way deciduous trees lose their leaves. Evergreen needles fall off a few at a time, leaving many needles on the tree throughout the year. This allows evergreen trees to do photosynthesis all through the year.

◀ Evergreen trees grow all around the world.

Can We Help Trees?

Trees help us in many ways. We need to care for them and help them live. Many people work hard to lower air and water pollution because it can make trees sick.

You can help trees by

○ recycling paper so we won't have to cut down so many trees

○ being careful at campsites to prevent fires

○ planting more trees

If we all work together, we can protect the world's trees.

Web Sites:

You can learn more about trees at this Web site:
http://wvweb.com/www/fall/leaves.html

Glossary

cambium (KAM-bee-um) The layer of cells between the bark and the sapwood that produces new growth.

carbon dioxide (KAR-bin dy-OK-syd) A gas that trees use to make food.

cells (SELZ) Tiny units that make up all living things.

chlorophyll (KLOR-uh-fil) A green coloring in leaves that makes them able to use energy from sunlight to make food.

deciduous (deh-SIH-joo-us) A type of tree that loses its leaves in fall.

heartwood (HART-wood) The wood core that supports a tree.

ingredients (in-GREE-dee-ints) Nutrients that combine to form the food of a tree.

lumber (LUM-ber) Wood from a tree that is used for building.

mineral (MIH-ner-ul) A natural ingredient from Earth's soil, such as iron or potassium.

oxygen (AHK-sih-jen) A gas present in air that is necessary for people and animals to breathe.

photosynthesis (foh-toh-SIN-thuh-sis) The process in which leaves use energy from sunlight, gases from air, and water from soil to make food and oxygen.

ripe (RYP) When something is ready to eat or use.

root (ROOT) The part of a tree that grows down into the ground.

sapwood (SAP-wood) A living part of a tree inside the trunk that carries water up from the roots.

Index